Amarnath Yatra

The Story to the Abode of God & The Secret of Immortality

Joydeep Roy

Copyright © Joydeep Roy
All Rights Reserved.

This book has been self-published with all reasonable efforts taken to make the material error-free by the author. No part of this book shall be used, reproduced in any manner whatsoever without written permission from the author, except in the case of brief quotations embodied in critical articles and reviews.

The Author of this book is solely responsible and liable for its content including but not limited to the views, representations, descriptions, statements, information, opinions and references ["Content"]. The Content of this book shall not constitute or be construed or deemed to reflect the opinion or expression of the Publisher or Editor. Neither the Publisher nor Editor endorse or approve the Content of this book or guarantee the reliability, accuracy or completeness of the Content published herein and do not make any representations or warranties of any kind, express or implied, including but not limited to the implied warranties of merchantability, fitness for a particular purpose. The Publisher and Editor shall not be liable whatsoever for any errors, omissions, whether such errors or omissions result from negligence, accident, or any other cause or claims for loss or damages of any kind, including without limitation, indirect or consequential loss or damage arising out of use, inability to use, or about the reliability, accuracy or sufficiency of the information contained in this book.

Made with ❤ on the Notion Press Platform

www.notionpress.com

"When GOD gave men tongues, he never dreamed that they would want to talk about the Himalayas; there are consequently no words in the world to do it with".

– **Sara Jeannette Duncan**

Dedication:

I dedicate this book to all those pilgrims who died in the terrorist attack in Anantnag district when they were returning after visiting the holy shrine. Such cowardly act only make us more determined that we won't bow down by such terrorist attacks.

Acknowledgement:

I owe this book to so many people who have directly or indirectly influenced me in my journey of writing this book.

I thank my maternal uncle Rintu; who travelled along with me and showed extreme willpower and courage to complete the trek gracefully.

I want to thank all the people with whom I have interacted in the trail for the motivation and support extended to me, especially the Indian Army personnel who were exceptional in maintaining law and order other than helping the pilgrims in whatever way possible and always with a smiling face.

Preamble:

It was always there in my wish list but could never materialize because of whatsoever reason. So when the first notification of the Yatra came, it was almost like a conscious decision of now or never. Once that's done, the rest is the usual process of getting the medical checkup and the permit formalities. Initially, it was planned for a solo trip but when my Mama came to know about this, it was like "it has to be a Mama Bhanja combined effort". So, here our journey begins....

We started with a curfew ☹ :

So, the Yatra date has been fixed on 9th July, from Pahalgaon Base camp. Till 8th morning everything was 'fit and fine' till the time we came across this post in the "Times of India" just before boarding the Srinagar bound flight at 7.25 am.

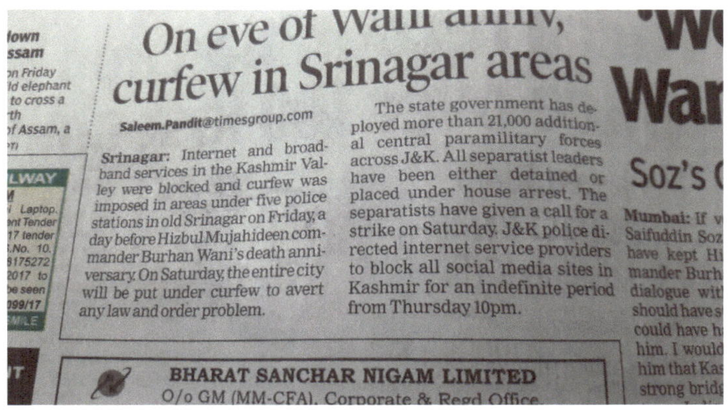

Some immediate calls to some acquaintances at Jammu couldn't give us any hope; so we landed "Sheikh-ul-Alam Airport" at Srinagar at scheduled time with a curfew outsideL. The JKTDC representative at the airport made it clear that travel to Pahalgaon is not at all advisable in that curfew and even if any private operator want to take us, the Army may not allow as the route passes through Anantnag District, which is the birthplace of the notorious Mujahidin commander Wani and the curfew is all about ensuring peace in the valley on his 1st death anniversary. So, we were left out with no other option but to stay back at Srinagar.

Temporary shelter in a Guest House @ Srinagar

It was just a sheer coincidence that I got in touch with an old acquaintance based in Jammu and he could arrange one Guest House at a high security area situated just outside the main airport gate. The owner was a young guy by the name 'Riaz' and he ensured that we would get the best possible hospitality. The striking features of the houses in that complex were the beautiful lawns and the different type of ornamental plants they maintain inside the terrace.

Riaz only arranged a car for an early morning startup for Pahalgaon as we had to reach the Chandanwari gate before 11 am.

Alarm set @ 3am, 9ᵗʰ July

After the alarm rang at 3 am, I was just wondering whether the decision of starting at such an early hour would be correct or not, Mama just exclaimed "Jai Bhole – Jo hoga dekha jayega". After this, no one can remain at bed and we were almost ready by the time the reminder alarm started rumbling at 3.20 am.

The Traveira reported just on time and we set our journey to the abode of GOD exactly at 3.30 am from Srinagar.

The journey was uneventful, and we were too scared to take any breaks in between. Not even any photos…

Pahalgaon – Love at First site

While the early morning sun came slinking, the trees and the meadows had yet to wake up when we reached Pahalgaon. If someone ask me "How green was the valley?" I don't think I would be able to answer. It's not the same green which I have seen in Ghats after the monsoon, it's not the same which I have seen in dooars; it's something different. If someone wants to see the combination of breathtaking vistas of meadows and the snow clad Himalayan Mountains – Pahalgaon is the place. No wonder why Kashmir is called the Heaven on earth.

Pahalgaon to Chandanwari is only 16 km and usually takes 30 mins. We booked a Maruti Van which charged Rs 600/– to drop us there. The view of the valley was breathtaking with Lidder river flowing at full might. Dense evergreen forest jotted the slope of the mountains and an occasional peck of the snow clad peaks far away took away all the anxiety of the last 3 hours' drive. The famous Betab valley came into sight just after few kms; no wonder that one of the most romantic Hindi film in the early 80's was shot here only.

As per Hindu mythology, when Lord Shiva decided to share the secret of immortality with Maa Parvati in the holy cave, at first they reached Pahalgaon. Pahalgaon stands for "Village of the shepherds"; however, the local Kashmiris believed that Pahal means "Bull". So, Lord Shiva left his Nandi (The Bull which he used to ride) at Pahalgam (Bail gaon) and at Chandanwari removed Moon from hairs (Jataon) before proceeding towards the Holy cave.

"Ghoda Chahiye?" – @ Chandanwari Entry

Even before we could come out from the van, at least 6 – 7 people surrounded us for hiring a horse. Everyone claimed that their horse was actually a "horse" and not a "pony". Some of them took it to the extent that his horse had acted in films like "Bajrangi Bhaijaan" and "Haider" and both Sallu and Shahid Bhai had taken a ride on that horse. Since it was already decided that mama would take a horse, we finally hired the horse which had acted in the climax scene of the "Bajrangi Bhaijaan". We thought of not ignoring the "horsepower" blessed by Sallu Bhai ☺. Although Government has a fixed rate for the horses but in reality it's all about negotiation at site.

There were almost 3 security check in points by both Indian Army and JK police. The security arrangement was very tight, might be because of the continuous threat from the militant outfits. Finally, we started our journey exactly at 8.30 am after having a quick breakfast at one of the langars just after the entry gate.

One of the most notable feature of the Amarnath Yatra was the hospitality of the bhandaras/langars all across the trail. The snacks served by them along with steaming hot tea and accompanied with an everlasting smile on their face was one of the key takeaways of the Amarnath Yatra.

The stiff climb from the start itself...

Chandanwari (9500 ft) to Pissu Top (11000 ft) was approximately 3 kms and was a difficult ascent. It's also considered to be the most challenging part of the yatra. This might be because of the fact of sudden change in the acclamation of the body. Also, if someone started thinking that he had to walk up so much height, the psychological changes also made the body tired. The altitude gain was almost 1500 ft. in this 3 kms stretch. The trail was well defined with no major difficulty other than the stiff zig zag turns along the same face of the mountain.

Pissutop is the place where Lord Shiva left all his poisonous creatures like "Pissus" or scorpions from his body. It is also said that in order to reach first for darshan of Bhole Nath, there was a war between Devtas and Rakshas. With the power of Shiv, devtas could kill the rakshas in such large number that the heap of their dead bodies had resulted in a high mountain called Pissu Top. I don't know how many Rakshas died during that war but had it been some more, I doubt how many of us would have been able to cross the Pissu Top.

By the time I reached Pissu top it was 9.40 am; little more than an hour from Chandanwari. It's like a small plateau in between two ridges. Another striking feature was the absence of any trees at the top. What I understood, when Shiva and Parvati reached Pissu Top, there was a very thick forest there and Parvati was lost in the forest. Shiva ordered the jungle to find Parvati, but the jungle failed to do that. So Shiva opened his third eye and burnt the jungle. So from that time onwards, no tree can grow at the top.

There were at least 3 bhandaras at Pissu Top serving hot parathas, chat and rice meal. I could even see one Momo counter in one of them. Mama was already enjoying food at a bhandara when I reached there. Since he was already rejuvenated by hot samosas and pakoras; at some point of time, Mama started dancing with the beats of the Bhakti songs. Initially he started with devotional dance steps but quickly clubbed Mithunda's disco dancer steps with equal ease. On special request, those photos are not posted here 😊.

Easy trail to Zoji Bal

Pissu Top to Zoji bal is approximately 3 kms and more or less a flat trail. There was as such no altitude gain in this stretch. However, the landscape started changing significantly after Pissu Top since we had already come out from the tree zone. The weather was wonderful with clear sky. Temperature also dipped a little bit as the trail was passing through a gorge; with steep rocky walls on the left and the might lidder river on my right.

It took me less than an hour to reach Zoji Bal inspite of the fact that I took frequent breaks for taking photographs and to enjoy the sheer beauty of the inner Himalayas. There were couple of Bhandaras at Zoji bal also.

Straight rocky walk to Naga koti

Distance between Zojibal and Nagakoti is approximately 2 km and have moderate climb. The altitude increases by 300 ft. only. The best part of this trail was the beautiful mountain streams on the other side of the Lidder river connecting to the main stream.

Till the last 500 mtrs, the trail was on a dry rocky road, so one wouldn't find it hard walking on that. However, at one point the trail took a turn with a little descent and then again a substantial ascent. There is a beautiful waterfall at this point and I could see lot of people taking selfies from different angles. Infact, all across the trail, I had seen lot of selfie maniacs; sometimes it looked dangerous by the way they would stand in front of a cliff and click.

Also, the trail became quite narrow and rocky going forward, so yatris who were on horses were asked to get down at this point and go by walking till Naga koti. As per Hindu mythology, it is here in Nagakoti where Lord Shiva started to leave poisonous snakes from his body.

On the way to the Jewel of Mother nature – The Seshnag Lake

Initially, I thought of waiting for Mama to come and then we would go to Seshnag together; but with no sign of him for the next 10-15 minutes, I decided to move forward towards Seshnag; our destination for Day 1 camping.

Seshnag is approximately 3 kms from Naga koti and the altitude difference is only 400 ft. So, not too much of hard walking on the trail.

The beauty of the trail was the stiff mountain slopes on both sides and the opening up of the valley facing towards some high altitude peaks.

After 1 km from Naga koti, I could see the first view of the lake. It took me few seconds to absorb the beauty of it from that distance. It was like a small light green colored water body appearing between two small hills. With the sky being absolutely clear, the sight of the Seshnag lake and the spectacular scenery around it gave me a feeling of having been lifted to a heaven.

Once I started coming closer to the lake, the surrounding mountain peaks started opening up and it was a sight that I would never forget in my life. The famous trinity peak by the name "Brahma, Vishnu and Maheshwar" was in full view at the background.

As per Hindu mythology, Seshnag means the king of snakes and the lake was dug by Seshnag himself when Lord Shiva released him in this place from his hair. It is also believed that Seshnag is still living in this lake. Also, Seshnag is the one who was incarnated as Lakshmana, the younger brother of Lord Rama in Treta Yuga and also as Balram the elder brother of Lord Krishna in Dwapara Yuga. The seven mountains around the lakes are called 7 hoods of the Seshnag serpent. According to Rajtarangni, there is another lake just above seshnag which is known as zamturnag (son-in-law of Seshnag).

Seshnag lake is fed by the melted snow from the surrounding mountains. Further, the water joins the Lidder river in Pahalgam valley. Seshnag is also an oligotrophic lake that means it has low primary productivity, the result of low nutrient content. These lakes have low algal production, and consequently, often have very clear waters, with high drinking water quality. The bottom waters of such lakes typically have ample oxygen, thus, such lakes often support many fish species, like trout, which require cold, well-oxygenated waters.

@ Seshnag – End of Day 1

There are camps nearby Seshnag lake where one can get tents for the night stay. The rate is already fixed by the government. It was 1.30 in the afternoon when I reached the camping site. I had walked almost 16 kms starting from Chandanwari in 5 hours. Although the gateway to Panchtarni was open, it was already decided that we would stay here for the night.

Mama reached almost at the same time. We found a decent 4 man's tent and shared with one more group (father son duo) whom we had met at Pahalgaon.

The tents were reasonably clean and well maintained. Nevertheless, one shouldn't expect any luxury at this altitude and terrain. Infact, we could even found few locals arranging warm water if someone wanted to have a quick bath.

There were at least 5 – 6 bhandaras serving hot food throughout the day. In one of the bhandara we found Panipuri's which were not only fresh but crispy too. I really don't know how they could manage this at such a terrain and hostile climatic conditions. We were really overwhelmed with their warm hospitality which made our journey more memorable.

India Pakistan Cricket Match @ Seshnag International Stadium 😊

After a nice meal at one of the bhandara, I was strolling around when I came across a small helipad at one corner of the camping site; towards the CRPF camp. Interestingly, a game of cricket was about to start and it looked like some of the Yatris were also taking part along with locals. I couldn't resist the temptation and approached them for taking me in a team which they gladly obliged. On a later stage, I realized that all the yatris had been categorized as Indian team and the locals were representing Pakistan. It sounds odd but true. Infact, throughout the trail I could felt a mild discomfort between the yatris and the locals which were not very usual in this route as understood from different blogs.

I must say, playing a cricket match in such an ambience was extremely fulfilling. With Trinity peak clearly visible on one side, I tried to field somewhere near the deep square leg so that I could get a decent view of the peaks. The pictures say it all.

The match ended in draw; not because of the fact that the score became equal but for the reason that the 'only' ball got lost somewhere in the maze of tents. The locals were not happy as they thought they would beat the Yatris or 'India'; however the fact was that India was in a much better situation to win had the match continued.

"Never waste any amount of time doing anything important when there is a sunset outside that you should be sitting under!" – C. JoyBell C.

On the way to Mahagunas (Ganesh) Top – to give company to Lord Ganesh 😊 – Day II

There are couple of golden rules in hiking/trekking.

1. **Any walking pace faster than your own natural ability (golden pace) would tire the person out**

2. **Start early and end early.**

This is very much applicable especially when one is crossing high altitude pass like Mahagunas.

I found this extract from India hikes website very useful for highlighting the importance of this thumb rule...

"Every person has a natural rhythm and pace in their walk. I call this the golden pace. This is normally independent of their athletic ability. I have friends are marathon runners but when it comes to walking, their golden pace is a mere 5 km per hour. They can certainly walk faster as they are fit.

*However, **any walking pace faster than the golden pace would tire the person out** quickly. A tired body is predisposed to altitude sickness.*

If one walks at the golden pace, there should be no breathlessness, no feeling of exhaustion and only mild sweating. If any of these are felt, the pace is not good for that person.

Climbing and trekking are considered to be lonely sports. There are no prizes or victories. It is about the experience. Yet I have seen that trekkers very often get subconsciously psyched into meaningless races and timings".

This is very much applicable for Amaranth Yatris also especially for the Seshnag to Mahagunas trail as it was the highest altitude point of the Amarnath yatra.

We started from Seshnag at around 5 am with a mindset of completing the darshan on the same day itself. Also, being the first Monday of the "Shraban" month, it's considered to be auspicious.

After sometime, the sun began to peak behind a peak and gradually illuminated the surrounding mountains. For about the first few minutes, all the mountains appeared to look the same, till the time the sun had risen enough to illuminate the beauty of the surroundings. We were literally at the top of the world, reminded me the song "aaj mein upar aasman neeche…"

"How glorious a greeting the sun gives the mountains" – John Muir.

Due to melting of snow, the track from Seshnag to Mahagunas had become quite slippery. It was almost a straight trail with not much elevation gain till the first 1 km.

Thereafter, we had to cross the river and came towards the left side of the valley and from there onwards the trail became quite steep and rocky. And with horses moving across in large numbers, which made my movement slow.

The snow covered, white and shining, Himalayas inspire to stand tall and rigid. The nature makes you feel so tiny before it that you become humble. The bold and breathtaking trail to the safe heaven keeps the blood streaming into your heart.

The first resting point towards Mahagunas is the Warbal top which is approximately 3 kms from Seshnag and at 13800 ft height. So, it's almost a 2000 ft gain in altitude within 3 kms!

This was almost similar to climbing Pissu top climb but the lack of oxygen at this altitude made it difficult.

By the time I reached Warbal Top, it was almost 7 am. Both CRPF and Indian Army had set up small medical camps for the Yatris who were complaining about altitude sickness. The remaining 1.5 kms to Mahagunas pass is a rocky trail with a gradual ascent. Mahagunas or Ganesh Top (14500 ft) is the highest point of the Yatra. It is a pass in between two peaks which connects two mountain ranges. As per Hindu mythology, it is believed that at this place, Ganesha was left behind as Lord Shiva didn't want anybody else other than Maa Parvati to listen the holy secret of immortality. Hence, this place is named as Ganesh Top. Now, standing at the top of the pass, I realized that though we human beings are considered to be the most advanced of all living beings on earth, still we are very insignificant in front of the mighty Himalayas. *"In simple words, we are insignificant even when we claim that we have conquered the highest of the mountains, deepest of the seas and thickest of the forests. Nature is incomprehensible and it is better not to meddle with it."*

Roasted Malai chap @ Poshpatri 😊

Poshpatri (14000 ft) is just 1.5 kms from Mahagunas pass and is almost a flat trail. Infact, it was much relief to the knees after that steep climb to Mahagunas Top. The landscape is awesome. It's more like that of human emotions. With every turn, it changes. These changing moods of the nature make the mountains so vibrant and imposing. As Frank Smythe once said *"There is something about the Himalayas; something unseen and unknown, a charm that pervades every hour spent among them, a mystery intriguing and disturbing. Confronted by them, a man loses his grasp of ordinary things, perceiving himself as immortal, an entity capable of outdistancing all changes, all life, all death.*

"I reached Poshpatri at around 8 am and could find Mama already had his platter full with 'Navratan Pulao and 'roasted malai chap' in the "Shree Shiva Sevak Delhi" bhandara. What I understood, they arrange bhandara every year at Poshpatra and prepare more than 50 items every day for bhog and langar.

We could even find ice cream, different type of fruit juices and meetha pan!! No doubt, this was the best Bhandara in the entire Yatra trail.

The foot massager @ Panchtarni!!

After crossing the Mahagunas Top and couple of glaciers, the trail passes through vast rolling green meadows. The surrounding mountain slopes now had again some green patches of grass, giving it a fresh look. There were bubbly streams and some small waterfalls passing across the trail. I could see herds of pashmina and goats grazing in the slopes of the green meadows. I somehow realized that this is the place where time does stand still. One can appreciate the beauty of nature as long as he wants, even one can reach out to the glaciers and touch it. Personally, I would always recommend to take the Pahalgaon route for the Amarnath Yatra to all the trek enthusiasts.

The trail from Poshpatri to Panchtarni is approximately 8 km and is almost a steady descend as its altitude is less than that of Poshpatri by almost 1500 ft. Infact, just before reaching Panchtarni, the trail suddenly dropped to some few hundred feet's and ended up in a vast valley where one could see the five streams flowing at the base of Mount Bhairav.

As per Hindu mythology, Lord Shiva left the five elements (Earth, Water, Air, Fire and Sky), which constitutes the living beings, behind at Panchtarni. So, on reaching here, one can see a river split in 5 parts in the plain which are originated from Lord Shiva's hair (Jata).

Panchtarani is very crowded; may be because of the fact that this is the last camping point (although one can stay at Sangam/near Holy cave) before one starts for the Holy cave which is approximately 6 kms from there. The helicopter service operates from there only for Yatris who wants to come by air.

Here, I must convey my sincere gratitude to both Indian Army, CRPF and J&K police. They do a remarkable job every year in controlling the huge crowd amidst all the security threats and hostile weather.

When I reached Panchtarni, it was 11 in the morning and I had enough time to proceed and complete darshan today itself. At Poshpatri only, Mama and I decided to meet near the camp site near Holy cave; so I decided not to look out for Mama at Panchtarni; although I was sure that I could get him at one of the bhandaras 😊.

Its only dust towards Sangam

While starting from Chandanwari base camp, I had noticed some people selling face masks; but didn't pay much attention as I couldn't make out for what purpose it would be required. I came to realize the importance of the face musk once I started for Sangam from Panchtarni. Almost the entire stretch is rocky, extremely dusty and in some areas it's so narrow and dangerous that accidents can happen anytime if someone is not careful enough. Added to the agony is the large number of horses and ponies which walk in parallel along with the yatris. One must be extremely careful to avoid a collision with the horses and dandies. I personally strongly recommend to put a time based control here by the authority.

Sangam or Sangam top is a place where the routes of Pahalgam and Baltal meet. Apart from this; it's also the confluence of two streams coming from two different directions. The Amarnath Cave is just 3 kms away from the Sangam.

Barfani Baba darshan @ Holy cave – Day II

The Holy Cave is situated in a narrow gorge at the farther end of Lidder Valley, Amarnath Shrine stands at approx 3,900 m. The holy cave is the abode of Lord Shiva who is enshrined in the form of an ice-lingam in this cave. This lingam is formed naturally, which is believed to wax and wane with the moon, although there is no scientific evidence for this belief. There are total three lingas over there. It's believed that the biggest linga represented lord Shiva, other two for goddess Parvati and Shri Ganesh.

As per Hindu Mythology, this is the cave where Lord Shiva narrated the secret of immortality to Maa Parvati. To ensure that no living being is able to listen to the secrets, Lord Shiva created Rudra named Kalagni and ordered him to spread fire to eliminate every living thing in and around the holy cave. After this he started narrating the secret of immortality to Parvati. But as a matter of chance, one egg which was lying beneath the deer skin remained protected. It was believed to be nonliving and more over it was protected by Shiva – Parvati Asan (bed). The pair of pigeons which were born out of this egg became immortal after listening to the secret of immortality (Amar katha). Since then the holy place came to be known as Amarnath, and every year on the full moon day of Shravan, a pair of pigeons is seen inside the cave.

The other legend says that a parrot hatched from egg and heard the Amar Katha. While Shiva was narrating the Amar Katha, Parvati happened to fall asleep and it was actually the parrot which was making the responses. Therefore Shiva was under the impression that Parvati was listening to the story.

However when he finished narration, he realized that Parvati was actually asleep and it was the parrot which had listened to the story. This infuriated Shiva, who sent his trident to kill the parrot. To escape the trident, it is believed that the parrot entered a lady, who was wife of a sage and started to grow inside her womb.

However since it had already listened to the Amar Katha, it did not want to be born in a world full of Maya (illusion). Therefore even after the baby was due, it did not come out and the sage's wife was in great distress. The sage then prayed to Brahma, who told the sage the reason why the baby was not coming out. He also advised the sage to approach Vishnu, the Lord of Maya, to temporarily rid the world of Maya so that the baby would come out.

Accordingly the sage approached Vishnu and Vishnu removed Maya from the world temporarily. The baby which was born was called Shuka (Shuka in Sanskrit means parrot) and he grew up to become a famous sage "Sukhdev".

After this incident, Shiva ordained that anybody who listened to the Amar Katha or who visits the Amarnath cave will attain moksha (Freedom from the cycle of birth and death)." I reached near the base of the cave at 2 pm. The weather was clear and I could clearly see the serpentine queue for the darshan. The opening of the cave is quite large. One has to climb more than 400 stairs to reach near the lingam. The view around the cave is quite unique, surrounded by serrated jagged mountains.

All the makeshift arrangements near the holy cave like tents, bhandaras and shops are built on the surface of the glacier above the river. There are many places where the river has come out from the glacier surface and again has gone under it giving it an appearance of a snout.

The Yatra committee don't allow Yatris to take anything along with them for the darshan other than Prasad. One can buy Prasad from any one of the shops at the base of the cave and keep the remaining stuffs there including camera. The shopkeeper in turn gives a receipt, with the bag number and items clearly mentioned on it.

Just before entering the main gate, the queue had become quite dense, and I found it quite difficult to move forward because of devotees virtually crawling in the remaining steps. While I don't have any grudge against someone's religious beliefs but personally I don't find any justification in doing so. It's strictly my personal view with no intention of hurting anybody's religious sentiments. After some time and much effort, I could finally make my way to the temple verandah. The lingam is well protected inside a metal fence and from a distance I could make out it to be at least 9-10 ft in height. The energy of the place was so divine and powerful that I realized why so many people wanted to do Amarnath Baba darshan. This is one of those special moments where one could actually resonate with the divinity of the place. These were the moments which molded people to become better human beings. We meditated there for couple of minutes and came out from the cave with a sense of fulfillment. Mama was also very happy and satisfied that we had done darshan without any disturbance caused by bad weather or mountain sickness. He also made a promise to come back again next year...

Discussion with Arif mian @ Holy cave base camp

Since it was already 4 pm when we had completed the darshan, we decided to take the night halt at Holy cave camp site only. It started raining which made the road very slippery and dangerous. We took shelter in a tent owned by Arif Lone, a young Kashmiri and a recent college pass out. He had put up a tent at the base camp to help his father who in turn is a businessman dealing with puja materials and local handicrafts.

We settled down inside the tent as it started raining heavily outside. Arif Mian seemed to be quite enthusiastic and had updated knowledge on domestic and world politics. When he proactively raised the topic on J & K dispute with Pakistan, I thought it would be a good opportunity to understand the sentiments of Kashmiri youth's straight from the horse's mouth. He was quite aware of the fact that legally, Jammu and Kashmir is an integral and inseparable part of India and also why a plebiscite cannot be held today to find out a solution. However, some leaders intentionally misguided and convinced the kashmiris about the glorious victories of Islam. They were then determined to take up gun and force Indian people to leave the valley. However, at present, most of the Kashmiri youths are disillusioned and have stopped fighting and killing but are still called terrorists, when actually those fighting are mainly from POK, Pakistan and Afghanistan.

While I couldn't completely agree with his version but felt that it would be good not to linger it further because religion is one subject which I really don't believe. For me, its humanity which matters and not religion. In my last two days trek, I have seen lots of hard core Hindus (don't ask me how I make it out) getting carried out in dandies by Muslims…

With nothing much to do, we decided to take a quick stroll to the nearby tents when we came to know that some terrorists had fired on a bus and killed many yatris. The news completely rattled us. Lots of rumors started coming. With no network available, things became quite messy. Luckily, Mama was carrying a postpaid BSNL number (which was working intermittently in the last two days) which actually saved us in this turmoil. At least we could inform the family members about our whereabouts.

After this, suddenly we could sense a discomfort among the locals. Arif also moved out from the tent and came back only at late hours. With cold temperature setting in after the rain, we decided to give it for the day and went for a well-deserved sleep. I walked almost 19 kms today ☺.

A quick retreat to Baltal – Day III

We wake up much before dawn and started preparing ourselves for Baltal. It was dark outside. Yesterday's news of terrorist attack not only made the valley tensed but it made our program haywire as the news came of road blockage and curfew in some parts of the valley.

This time Mama took a horse who had not acted in any film so far😊. He didn't even negotiate the rate but put a condition that he would go down at the same pace as that of mine. After crossing the sangam, the stalls and shops left behind and now only high mountains were all around. The pictures say it all...

The gas stand @ Barari

As per Wikipedia "Jugaad refers to an innovative fix or a simple work-around, a solution that bends the rules, or a resource that can be used in such a way. It is also often used to signify creativity—to make existing things work, or to create new things with meager resources." I believe, one of the best example can be this; gas cylinders plunged under the ground so that they couldn't roll out because of the slope.

The "Red" omelet @ Baltal Base camp

We got stuck at Baltal for the day as it was almost 11 am and army was not allowing any vehicle to move out of Baltal after 9am because of the ongoing curfew. We were left out with no other option but to hire a tent. The weather suddenly became hostile with thunderstorm and rain. While moving around the main Bus stand for arranging a cab for next day's journey to Srinagar, I could see one of the yatri eating an omelet. The color of the omelet completely knocked me out. How an omelet could be so red!! On digging into the details, I could find out that there is no proportionate rule applicable here and the percentage of red chilies overweighs than any other ingredients...

Epilogue

"All the GODs, all the heavens, all the hells, are within you" – Joseph Campbell

Himalaya is an institute; which can teach us the best learnings of our life. Beautiful snow clad mountains, breathtaking views, hospitable locals, centuries old culture; these are just some of few reasons on why one should come to Himalayas at least once in their lifetime. It gives a realization that how insignificant our lives are. It makes us realize that there are things beyond material wealth. In Himalayas, the landscape varies as much as human emotions. Once someone starts spending time with the Himalayas, it no longer behaves like a mountain range. It becomes a part of our life; stories of the time we spent at some of these places. So, if you are a traveler, then you must visit Himalayas. You must see the mountains.

The amaranth yatra, they say, leaves a profound impact of spiritual adoration on the minds of the pilgrims, who stride through an exceedingly enchanting and enthralling route to meet the shinning glory and greatness of GOD. This yatra is a reminder that the path to salvation involves struggle and stamina. This is a place where all religions, all teachings are getting synthesized. Swami Vivekananda recounting his amaranth experience said "I have never been anything so beautiful, so inspiring."...

And finally, it's about the journey, not the destination. The journey reminded me once again that there is so much beauty in this world to be explored and experienced. So embrace and enjoy.

Now, after completing writing this, I called up Mama and narrated the write-up; he said "Bhanja, that was one hell of a trip. But we will go again. Har har Mahadev". And that's the spirit of Himalayas...

References:

https://www.ghumakkar.com/amarnath-yatra-pissutop-sheshnag/

https://www.ghumakkar.com/amarnath-yatra-pishutop-zajipal-nagakoti/

https://www.tripoto.com/trip/amarnath-trek-to-salvation-5752dda21992e

https://iitbmountaineering.wordpress.com/2011/03/13/story-of-amarnath/

http://amarnath2010.blogspot.in/

http://www.amarnathyatra.org/legend.htm

http://sandeepachetan.com/amarnath-yatra-on-foot-pahalgam/

PLACE	ALTITUDE		DISTANCE	FROM
	MTRS	FEET		
CHANDANWARI	2895	9500	16.0 KM	PAHALGAM
PISSU TOP	3377	11000	3.0 KM	CHANDANWARI
SHESHNAG	3352	11730	11.0 KM	PISSU TOP
MAHAGUNAS	4276	14000	4.6 KM	SHESH NAG
PANCHTARNI	3657	12000	9.4 KM	MAHAGUNUS TOP
SANGAM	–	–	3.0 KM	PANCHTARNI
HOLY CAVE	3952	13000	3.0 KM	SANGAM

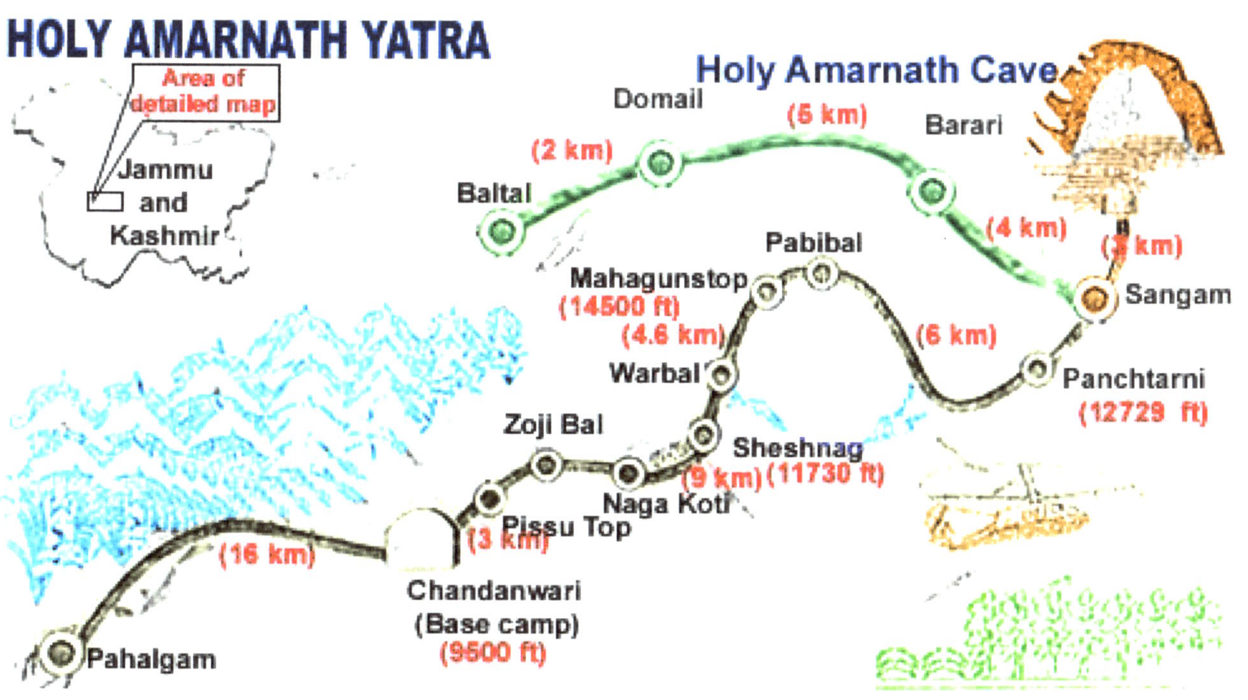
HOLY AMARNATH YATRA
Area of detailed map
Jammu and Kashmir
Holy Amarnath Cave
Domail
Barari
(5 km)
(2 km)
Baltal
(4 km)
(3 km)
Sangam
Pabibal
Mahagunstop (14500 ft)
(6 km)
Panchtarni (12729 ft)
Warbal
(4.6 km)
Zoji Bal
Sheshnag (11730 ft)
(9 km)
Naga Koti
Pissu Top
(3 km)
(16 km)
Chandanwari (Base camp) (9500 ft)
Pahalgam